For my father on the Otherside.

I will see you again; this is not where it ends.
~Carrie Underwood, Singer

ACKNOWLEDGMENTS 6
PREFACE 7
AUTHOR NOTE 8

INTRODUCTION: WHAT PEOPLE THINK OF UFOS AND ALIENS 10
Current Discussion of Time 15
Understanding a Concept 16

GETTING IN TOUCH WITH YOUR ALIEN 19
The Mind/Body/Spirit Approach: Your Personal Protection 30
What Can Go Wrong If You Don't Have Protection? 31
A Prayer to Michael 32

RELAXATION, INTERPRETATION, AND A BEAST OF BURDEN 36
Some Preliminaries 36
Preparing for Visualization 44
Relaxation 46
The Climb to Management 50
Management Interaction 51
The Way Back 53

RECORDING AND RESEARCHING YOUR EXPERIENCES 54
The Importance of Getting It as Exact as You Can 54
Form 54
Should You Report Your Experience? What's the Value? 55

UFO & ALIEN MANAGEMENT

A Guide to Discovering, Evaluating, and Directing Sightings, Abductions, & Contactee Experiences

DINAH ROSEBERRY

Schiffer Publishing Ltd®
4880 Lower Valley Road • Atglen, PA 19310

Other Schiffer Books By Dinah Roseberry

Ghosts of Valley Forge and Phoenixville, 978-0-7643-2633-2, $14.95
Cape May Haunts (with Laurie Hull), 978-0-7643-2821-3, $14.95
Spooky York, Pennsylvania (with Scott Butcher), 978-0-7643-3021-6, $14.99
Spooky Creepy Baltimore County, 978-0-7643-3254-8, $14.99
Psychic Pets: Solving Paranormal Mysteries, 978-0-7643-3398-9, $12.99
Ghost Hunters' Tool Kit (with Stuart Schneider), 978-0-7643-3912-7, $34.99
Animals Impacting the World (with Mary Gasparo), 978-0-7643-4237-0, $16.99

DISCLAIMER
Note that the methods described here provide no guarantee that you will be able to contact entities from other realms. There are some folks who are just not supposed to be involved with this kind of thing. The author and publisher take no responsibility for poor results due to ineffectively protecting your person, or for entities that break through your protection (for any reason including and especially a disbelief in God, guides, or angels). It is further noted that everyone will have a different experience and may not reflect the author's experiences. The author and publisher take no responsibility for the reader's interactions with UFOs or aliens or their particular experiences (including abduction, night terrors, visions, new abilities, sightings, unpleasant trips, etc.). Success may or may not be sporadic. During investigations and research we have experienced positive experiences and then there have also been times where silence or strange experiences have been the result.

Library of Congress Control Number: 2014932459

Designed by John P. Cheek
Cover design by Justin Watkinson
Type set in Parisian BT/Book Antiqua

Cover image: *Fantastic alpine landscape. Mountains in the moonlight* © Heizel.
Image by www.bigstockphoto.com.

Portrait of a young camel close-up isolated on white background © pzAxe.
Image by www.bigstockphoto.com.

ISBN: 978-0-7643-4606-4
Printed in China

Published by Schiffer Publishing, Ltd.
4880 Lower Valley Road
Atglen, PA 19310
Phone: (610) 593-1777; Fax: (610) 593-2002
E-mail: Info@schifferbooks.com

For our complete selection of fine books on this and related subjects, please visit our website at www.schifferbooks.com. You may also write for a free catalog.

This book may be purchased from the publisher. Please try your bookstore first.

We are always looking for people to write books on new and related subjects. If you have an idea for a book, please contact us at proposals@schifferbooks.com

Schiffer Publishing's titles are available at special discounts for bulk purchases for sales promotions or premiums. Special editions, including personalized covers, corporate imprints, and excerpts can be created in large quantities for special needs. For more information, contact the publisher.

CONTENTS

INSTIGATING AN EXPERIENCE 56

What Could Go Wrong? 56

What Won't You Allow? 57

Dreams 60

CONCLUSION 61

APPENDIX 62

Protection Prayer 62

Questions for Those Who Believe They Have Had an Experience 63

Questions for Those Who Do Not Believe They Have Had an Experience 64

Questions for Someone Who Remembers an Experience(s), But Finds Gaps in their Memories 65

Questions for Those Wishing to Confirm the Details of an Experience 66

The Relaxation Script 67

The Climb to Management Script 69

The Way Back Script 70

Troubleshooting 71

Case Study 1 73

Case Study 2 75

Form 77

RESOURCES 79

RECOMMENDED READING 80

ACKNOWLEDGMENTS

Anita Curtis

Barry & Connie Strohm

Beth Wilder

Betsey Lewis

Carroll Roseberry

Chris McClure

Darryl Anka

Debra Marshall

E. R. Vernor

Gerry & Joyce Medvec

Ginny Zaboronek

Jackie Wasdick

Jennifer Savage

John Cheek

Jordan Hofer

Justin Watkinson

Laurie Hull

(the late) Lee Prosser

Marge Richards

Nancy Leider

Pat Cassel

Pete & Nancy Schiffer

Preston Dennett

Richard Boylan

Sarah Tracy

Stacey McNutt

Stuart Schnieder

Tina Libby

Tracie Austin

Vicki Stong

The rest of the Schiffer Staff (always!)

PREFACE

UFO contact has often been described as a peak experience, one that affects the individual on multiple levels: physically, mentally, emotionally, and spiritually. While there have been many books written about UFO contact, almost nothing has been written about how to deal with it! Dinah's book is the first I've seen to put the experiencer first, and the aliens second.

The use of hypnosis is one method to recall missing time, but many people don't realize that there are other ways. If you are thinking about going under hypnosis to retrieve lost memories of a UFO encounter, I would recommend that you check out this book first.

When somebody tells me that they've had UFO contact and are considering hypnosis, I always urge them to try meditation first. While hypnosis is a valid tool to recover memories, it is not the only the way. Dinah's book provides a guided meditation that puts the experiencer in control of their experiences, allowing not only recall, but possible contact. Definitely a valuable book for anyone who is experiencing UFO contact.

PRESTON DENNETT

Preston Dennett is a field investigator for the Mutual UFO Network (MUFON), a ghost hunter, paranormal researcher, and author of over 14 books and more than 100 articles on UFOs and the paranormal. His articles have appeared in numerous magazines, including *Fate, Atlantis Rising, MUFON UFO Journal, Nexus, Paranormal Magazine, UFO magazine, Mysteries Magazine, Ufologist,* and others. He has appeared on radio and television programs and his research has been presented in the *L.A. Times, L.A. Daily News, Dallas Morning News,* and other newspapers. Preston has also taught classes on related subjects and lectures across the United States.

AUTHOR NOTE

Please remember as you read this book that there are little-known absolutes regarding UFOs and alien topics. While yes, it's true that a person can be put on death row for committing murder with less evidence than many have collected proving the existence of UFOs and related phenomena, the main body of decision-making powers have determined that it is, at this time, prudent to keep everyone from delving deeper into the subject in any way that would be beneficial to the disclosure of new (or known) data. Therefore, facts and theories become blurred and confusing. They mix with fictional ideals a bit, in some cases, as well as emotional remembrances, which can often inspire the brain to develop scenarios in exaggerated fashions. And, of course, as much as I hate to say this, there are those putting forth false evidence that merely shows a dedication toward having their fifteen minutes of fame.

One must dig through the rubbish. We in the believing, searching, and disclosure field of ufology already know these things. So I say all that to say that because of the discrepancies or gaps in our knowledge, please do not take what I write here as a replacement for any approved medical knowledge or cure for things that may have, or have not, happened to you while working in this field. Do not blindly traipse around UFO sighting areas without the appropriate safety precautions in place for doing so. Do not trespass on private property. There can be expensive fines or worse for such endeavors. And definitely do not believe so hard that an altercation with another individual believing the opposite thrusts you into an anger that can cause a stint in jail (or worse) for your actions.

Keep it simple. Know your own facts. Consider the gray areas. (Forgive the pun.) Make hypotheses. Try out the data. If it works for you, it was supposed to. (That's the old fate belief: "There's a time and place for everything." If it doesn't work for you, it wasn't supposed to. This could be for any number of reasons, including being for your own protection from a source higher than yourself.) Some things will ring true and you'll know in your heart that what you've experienced is real. Some things will clang like a broken cow bell. Those experiences, not so much.

So sit back and relax. Beyond research and learning a new method or two, I've written this book to help you manage your experiences (both before and after) in (hopefully) an enjoyable and compelling way. My motto in all things paranormal, body/mind/spirit, and ufology:

If something happens to you personally,
you know it's true.
Who cares what anyone else thinks?

INTRODUCTION
What People Think of UFOs and Aliens

Discovery News, in December of 2012 stated:

> A recent National Geographic Society poll reported that 36 percent of Americans—about 80 million people—believe UFOs exist; only 17 percent do not, and the rest of the people are undecided.

Now this 36 percent of Americans seems like a big number. National Geographic Society is not a group to *pooh pooh*. Yet…well, they never called me or anyone I know about this. So am I to think that there are 80 million people plus me (making it at least 80 million and 1) who believe that the world of ufology has some pretty big-clout numbers in the world?

Then there are the known UFO skeptics. Michael Shermer (from *Skeptical Inquirer*) says:

> Contrary to conventional wisdom, people of all levels of education like to believe in "weird things."

That's probably true, but I don't think he meant it in a good way. There are those (many if you read the numbers—but not 80 million plus 1 that *I* could find) out there who think the rest of us are ourselves weird and that we just like to believe in weird things. It makes us different—appalling to some and interesting to others.

Of course, if you bring into the mix formalized religion, have a shield with you—and maybe a spear or two—to protect yourselves

because people will quote to you religious texts relating how evil we (UFO believers) all are, how we invite the devil in. Their advice is to be careful what you do, and think, and believe, because they are pretty sure you're going to hell. Earplugs please. (And even if they're right, well, I just don't want to hear it.)

Since I'm mentioning religion, let me mention author and channeler Barry Strohm (along with channeler and psychic medium Barbara Lee) who quoted the Bible verse Zechariah 5:2 to the Master Guide Valentine (located on a Higher Plane) during a channeling session in 2013:

> Then I turned, and lifted up mine eyes, and looked, and behold a flying roll. And he said unto me, What seest thou? And I answered, I see a flying roll; the length thereof is twenty cubits, and the breadth thereof ten cubits.

The question to the guide was: *Was this an alien vehicle?*

The answer was:

– YES.

So, believe what you will, but there seem to be references to strange things in the bible and there are those of us able to channel varied beings who have the answers to the who and what of such matters. Whether you believe or not, it should pay dividends to at least keep your mind and ears open.

Renowned scientist Stephen Hawkings puts the "scare tactic" spin on aliens and UFOs. He told the *Huffington Post*:

> We only have to look at ourselves to see how intelligent life might develop into something we wouldn't want to meet. I imagine they might exist in massive ships, having used up all the resources from their home planet. Such advanced aliens would perhaps become nomads, looking to conquer and colonise whatever planets they can reach.

Yikes. It's *War of the Worlds* all over again. And listen, I'm not saying that his words may not be true. No one really knows for certain. It's all conjecture.

I could go on here giving quotes from presidents, astronauts, police officers, movie directors—people who have been touted as above reproach in their knowledge. I could even quote regular people like you and me. (Does that mean we can't be deemed above reproach?) You would hear any number of "truths." Some of those follow:

- There are no such things as UFOs.
- People who believe in UFOs are nuts.
- There *are* UFOs and they are coming to take our water, have sex with our people, eat us, enslave us, make us watch reruns of *Alf*. (Okay, aging myself here by bringing up retro *Alf*, but you really do have to watch it at least once just for perspective—just keep your cat away, if you do. Definitely buy a puppet.)
- There are UFOs and they are our friends, will cure cancer, have done, and will do, miracle healings, will talk to the "little people" (us) and not governments (them), will solve the Mother Earth problems facing our world, will visit us personally, will finally answer the question: why does the guy two seats down from me at the movies always have to go to the bathroom,

needing to crawl overtop me, during the very best scene in the show, thereby making that moment infuriating? They will tell us lots.

- There are UFOs and there aren't UFOs. And the middle road of belief: who cares? I don't know. Maybe, maybe not. (Just step back from me please if you don't have an opinion.)
- It's not a UFO. It's our governments playing yet another trick on us.
- It's a weather balloon, swamp gas, Chinese lanterns, someone's mother-in-law.

In truth, it doesn't matter if you believe or not. That doesn't change the truth one way or another. If a person does not believe and there really *are* strange alien crafts flying through our friendly skies, does that make those flying crafts any less real? If one *does* believe that there are such things as UFOs, does that make them truly there? You see, much like formalized religion and believing in God, just because you believe or don't believe, doesn't make either choice a truth. *It is what it is*. Period. It's just one person's (or 80 million people's) belief.

So for the first order of this book, I'd like you to suspend your belief or disbelief. The reason I ask this is because I'll be working with each person as an individual regarding their interactions with an otherworldly place (or places). Will mostly believers be reading this book? My guess is *yes*, but nonbelievers will get as much from the methods used here as a believer. (Unless the person is a raving disbeliever who daily stands on the soap box not believing in anything, much less ufology.)

What do people think of UFOs and Aliens?

I'm asking you to sit back and say: Who Cares?

But Will This Work?

As a caveat here, I'd like to tell you that the methods used here have worked for 99 percent of the people who have used it with my practice). The one person who did not glean success, had a hangover. (I suppose this may be the appropriate place to say that you should not be under the influence of anything when you try this. Not only will it skew your results, but I couldn't vouch for protective measures being in place in the way you will need them to be.)

One question that I always get (and had for myself in the beginning) is:

Why do some of the things I hear sound as though they are coming to me in my own voice rather than in an alien voice?

I don't really have a good answer for that, except that this is the way it is. There are some people who are already mediums, or psychic in some other way, who *do* hear other voices than their own. Most of us, however, are regular Joes and our brains don't allow varied communication. Much of what you will experience will be visual scenes narrated by your own voice. (Warning: do not listen or react to any negative message that puts another into harm's way. This kind of negativity is a red flag that your protections are not in place.)

So, the final statement before we begin:

*If you want to know, and truly are willing to follow the instructions and put in the time, this **WILL** work.*

CURRENT DISCUSSION OF TIME

Time is something that we must explore with greater gusto before we go into any true method of understanding UFOs or alien beings. This is not to say that one needs to entirely understand time concepts to have a positive experience (or a negative one—it can happen) or to be successful with methods used in this book, for many to this day, in the past, and in the future, will lead highly focused lives after traversing time in ways even *they* don't recognize or understand. Rather then, understanding concepts and the availability of an open mind become paramount for any individual or group summoning UFO experiences or remembrances of them, as we will be exploring here. Let us first examine why people (or humanity) choose to view time the way they/we do.

Because of the shell bodies that we all have, we are indeterminately linked to a time frame that is entirely "within." By that, I mean that there must be brain functions not currently allowing us to see time in any other fashion than linear. It is a must for daily life on our planet. Otherwise, how would you know that you were to be at work for a certain period during the day, sleep a prescribed amount of hours, etc. It has been quite some time since even a sparse interest in time could be viewed in a less linear fashion—i.e., the cave man did not plan to go to work. He merely went hunting when food was needed. He ate when he was hungry and time moved along or did not. It didn't matter. No one cared. In a society like humanity today, this method of just "allowing" is not practical. It has much to do with money, but that's another book entirely. Suffice it to say that currently, if you didn't have some constraints of linear time, most people would be shipped off to the local insane asylum. But wait, most of those have closed, so you would find those viewing time differently in the streets crazy if they could not buckle under the pressure of humanity's "time."

So what is time? Is it hours in a day? What is an hour? Is an hour a combination of minutes? What's a minute? What's a second? You see where I'm going, right? Can you identify and then describe exactly what the smallest measure of time is in any number of words or thoughts? Probably not. Scientific minds will describe time down to atoms or even smaller, I'm sure, but even they do not have the answer that goes deeper than some "alien" measurement that the normal folk would not understand, nor care to at this juncture.

Still, we rise to time; we move through our "time" with time. Much of our time experience (other than during sleep periods) is measured by activity. The things we do during the periods we call time give us the means to track how we live our lives. So if you experience one activity now, then another directly after the first, it feels as though you are moving forward in time. But are you? Does activity equal time? In the human experience, I'd have to say yes. But then that same equation has its own problems, for what is activity? The human mind cannot distinguish the connection entirely, but yet it is recognizable.

I was curious to see what the dictionary said relating to this conundrum and threw the word "time" into the search engine on dictionary.com. Usually, definitions from this site are quick and dirty. But under *time*, there were forty-one definitions from one source and sixty-one from another. Time is complicated.

UNDERSTANDING A CONCEPT

I decided to spend the day on the Internet to see if I could scientifically get my mind around this concept of time and the activities that moved it along. It was tough. It was in my mind to use some quotes, prove my point, and move forward. Not so easy, I'm afraid. I'd read, dismiss—if I don't understand this, how can I expect my readers to grasp it?—look some more, and finally ended up where I think I was supposed to be: reading about a person channeling a "star being" who could actually put things in language I could understand. Well, sorta kinda. I found bashar.org.

My first question was, who the heck was Bashar? And why would I take his explanation of time over a scientist's? Do mind/body/spirit people have the edge over science? You'll hear all kinds of answers to that question, but for our purposes, I'm choosing to say that science doesn't always get it right. And we don't know this until something they say is proven wrong. Horrible way to learn things. Anyway, back to Bashar. Channeler Darryl Anka describes his entity as an extraterrestrial friend who brings "a wave of new information that clearly explains in detail how the universe works and how each person creates the reality they experience."

Bashar (via Darryl) says:

> There is only **one moment** in the whole universe. Past, present, and future are all happening simultaneously **now**. What you perceive as the passage of time is actually you shifting your **perspective** (your consciousness) into parallel universes.

The example Darryl gives involves the movie *The Matrix*, and he shows the scene where the hero (played by Keanu Reeves) is fighting on the rooftop with Mr. Smith (the computer program). Mr. Smith fires a gun and we see the bullet in slow motion as "The One" (Keanu) bends over backwards at very uncomfortable angles to keep from being hit by the bullet, making movements that are astonishing and clearly required the help of special effects. Several camera angles are shown. Therefore, several perspectives of the same second can be viewed all at one time.

Still, though my mind "gets" the concept, as I sit looking at my husband while we are eating breakfast, I wonder how the medical procedure he'd endured the day before is really happening at the same time as we are eating the day after. That tells me that though I can read the words, but actually *living* the concept is a bit more daunting. I think aliens count on that as they come and go.

So, I'm thinking after all this research that understanding that there *is* a concept of time will be helpful. Once we employ the method of management that will occur later in this book, just a smattering of the time dilemma will be enough to suspend some of our preconceived fallacies. In other words, know that there is the concept, but then don't worry about it too much for now. It doesn't need to make sense until it does...

GETTING IN TOUCH WITH YOUR ALIEN

Channeler Nancy Lieder for the Zetas (some may know them as Grays, or Greys) at www.zetatalk.com reports that:

> The overall percentages [regarding alien life and life forms] are:
>
> - 1/1,000 planets that can sustain life.
> - 1/2,500 life-bearing planets that evolve intelligent species.
> - Of these,
>
>   75% are water babies,
>   15% are reptilian,
>   2.5 % are hominoid,
>   7.5 are bird like,
>   with an infinitesimal percentage of insect types.

Many find Nancy's channeling to be frightening. (Personally, I'm thinking of the infinitesimal percentage of insects. Please just shoot me now.) I feel it has a ring of truth—and yes, that surely makes it frightening. But whether one believes or not, it's best to be prepared, and that's the big message from this alien group, according to years of messages. These Zeta individuals warn of Planet X (or Nirubu) coming (also another book for another time). Whether one holds sway with this one way or another, taking about fifty hours (or more) to navigate all the information on this site will not be a waste of your time. (And yes, it will take fifty hours; this is not an exaggeration.)

I do need to note that other sources have said that the Zeta are not really telling the truth about things. To quote author and MUFON anthropology specialist Jordan Hofer, they are "dirty little bastards." What to believe is always the dilemma when researching alien topics.

For now, we will be looking at time—or the suspension of it—as we move into alien and UFO management, but before we begin that process, this method requires that you understand, or at least have an image in your mind, of who you will be dealing with as you undergo the process. While it's true that aliens may be a big part of this, there are other "entities" that could be part of your "trip." It may be that the other entities I discuss here really are aliens as well, or that aliens are really the other entities we peruse—and you just don't know; or you don't want to know. I hear you: What the *heck* is she talking about?

Many people undergoing this process method speak about angels, spirit guides, departed loved ones....Still others talk about Zeta aliens, Reptilians, and R2-D2. There is no shortage of entities that could be one thing or another. We simply don't know. Why? Well, it all goes back to the shell bodies and the brain with its limiting capability to ascertain realities. Not only can't we get our arms around time, but we also can't get around the perceptions of reality that we're shown that are outside our realm of reference. This includes seeing angels or guides or aliens, etc. I've heard people say that they've "seen" all these things. Some have actual visual experiences, others have the experience within the mind. (In the mind, by the way, is the way I experience these entities.) Whichever way one experiences an activity is right for that person, because they probably cannot grasp another—at least in a way that will allow them to manage the experience. Therefore, all interpretations are logical and acceptable at this point.

So, at this time, and through a variety of random investigations into the experiences of individuals, I will discuss some of what people deem acceptable visions of beings, according to their brains that will host you during your experiences. I will begin with my own major influence: Light Beings.

LIGHT BEINGS

These entities are usually seen within the mind, though some people have had visual experiences. They can be viewed as tall tubes of light. When I see them, the tubes have a golden and white aura fanning out in a manner that connects each tube to each other tube and beyond them as a whole, and there are usually five at a time. In meditation, they talk in one voice with the pronoun "We." There is always the impression of great, positive, loving light. The feeling when dealing with them mirrors teacher and student. But the teacher is so much grander and does not have negative personality traits, unlike the human teacher who, like all humans, has positive and negative aspects. It has been said by some that Light Beings are alien beings at a level so high that they are merely light and love. Others say they are angels and that this is just one way to view the angelic kingdom. (Which are they? One or the other? Both? That requires some out-of-the-box thinking, doesn't it?) I just had a recent notification from author Barry Strohm (*Haunting and History of the Battle of Gettysburg*) that during a channeling, he was told that my Light Beings were indeed angels. This was also imparted to me by authors and self-help instructors Ginny Zaboronek and Marge Richards.

ANGELS

Since we've talked about angels in the Light Being definition, it might be best to talk about the angel group next. There seem to be archangels (including Michael, Rafael, and many others) all tied to specific specialties. For example, one calls on Michael for protection and Rafael for healing (though these are not their only abilities). In the media, angels are drawn with great beautiful wings and features. They are mostly engulfed in white and golden light (like the Light Beings) and inspire feelings of love, safety, belonging, etc. People have seen them in reality and within the mind. A search on the Internet or at the library will tell you more specifics about angels than you'll ever be able to remember.

Guardian angels are a subgroup of angels and are often seen (in addition to the traditional way in visions) as entities disguised as humans or other Earthly creatures, here to provide some specific helping purpose for a particular individual at a certain time. People deep into the education surrounding angels will say that each of us at any given time can *be* a Guardian Angel for one another—that these things are destined and we have little control over an intense need to propel ourselves into a person's life just when they are in the most need. (I've had that happen to me on more than one occasion, so I know it's real.)

Satanic angels are another subgroup, but they are less describable, mainly because common brains don't like to look into corners where these "creatures" abide. Some call them demons, though others say that they are specifically related to, or in actuality are, Satan. Some say that Satan does not exist (and historic research does bear out some of this; see *I, Lucifer* by E. R. Vernor) and that it instead represents a negative thought form that we have personified. For this book and method, we will be dispelling any usage of information coming from this aspect, even if one has had prior dealings with it. Suffice it to say that any negative instruction to perform a negative task is not from a source we would want to encourage—real or not. Remember that perception is the understanding here. (Refrain from listening to dogs telling you to kill nurses. It never works out well for anyone.)

GUIDES

The guide group is huge and includes just about everything and everyone you can think of and I'm sure that many reading this book will be drawing from this group. Most identify their guides via deep meditation, or they "contract" (or ask) mediums, psychics, etc., to identify them. Many guides are of the Native American variety, found at one time in the Americas because that heritage draws heavily on the positive specifics of nature and living. They respect all life and manner of "being" down to, and including, inanimate objects. Though I've not had the experience of having a guide step forward that was inanimate, I have interacted with a rock (see *Psychic Pets: Solving Paranormal Mysteries*) and have learned that this was just one (if you'll forgive) stepping stone through the levels of understanding the universe. (It was a real surprise to me.) Additionally, anyone who has lived in the past who might have an influence on your life or care for you in some way can be a guide. The guide section might include prior psychics, painters, writers, "Native" individuals to varied tribal spirits around the world, historic figures, spiritual leaders, or regular people who have moved on to spirit lives. This also includes the spirits of deceased loved ones, though more often than not, these individuals only stay for a short time, before moving on to better circumstances (so I've heard and practically experienced—but there are always exceptions).

Though many don't like to hear this, ghosts can be guides—they too are individual spirits, but unfortunately, they are not often privy to the big picture and can give poor advice, however well meaning (so we will be dispelling help from them, too.)

Pets and animals, also, are noted as guides and give an entirely different perspectives to your experiences.

ZETA—THE GREYS

I begin the alien helpers with the Zeta, because they seem to be the premier entities talked about around the world and particularly in the United States. I'm inclined to say that there are some good and some bad, but I don't really know. I only know what I've personally experienced (good) and what I'm told from other experiencers (both good and bad). These entities are also called the Greys, though there are many varieties (just as we have many races of humanity). One reference I like to draw upon for vast information about the Zetas comes via channeler Nancy Lieder. In July of 1995, she channeled the Zeta, with them saying:

She [Nancy] *has met but few, as the Zetas are numerous in form. The forms result from the various planets we have spread to during the life of our form. Each planet plays upon the genetic structure, encouraging certain genetics to emerge and demonstrate their superiority in survival and longevity. Thus, the life form gradually adapts to the environment it finds itself in. Counts would differ, but for the sake of this discourse, we will say that the number of variations that would be visibly noticeable to humans is 127.*

Further, she goes on to channel about Zeta who are short skinny, tall skinny, pumpkin head, water, and others. They talk greatly about service-to-self and service-to-other mentalities. (For our purposes, those inviting Zeta interaction will be asking for service-to-others.) Why the name Zeta? From Nancy's channeling:

Zeta is your term for the star system we came from. [This would be Zeta Reticuli.] *Likewise, the Pleiadeans were named for their home constellation. Nancy adds, "They have the gray skin (because we can't really see the varied color structure that they have), the large almond dark eyes, slight skinny build, anywhere from three feet tall to seven feet."*

PLEIADEANS

As mentioned in the Zeta description, the Pleiadeans (also called Talls or Blonds) are named after a star system, the Pleades. This system is an open star cluster and is somewhere around 400 to 500 light years from earth. Discovery Education website says:

Light travels 186,000 miles per second. There are 60 seconds in a minute, 60 minutes in an hour, 24 hours in a day, and 365 days in a year. Multiply these together to get 31,500,000 seconds in a year. Multiply that times 186,000 miles per second and you get 5,850,000,000,000 miles—about 6 trillion miles.

[Multiply 6 trillion times 400 and figure how many miles at 60 mph (like in your car) and you have...well, "Are we there yet?" I'm tempted to say you can't get there from here—not in our generation anyway—or with any of our current travel modes, except your mind. That's the one we'll use.]

Just like with the Zetas, you will find many descriptions of this group that include Nordic features, angelic features, human features...they are a mixed bag, too. (Just like we are!) Mostly, you see lovely tall and fit blondish humanoid-looking beings with super positive attitudes. This is the group that is said to resemble most those of us we call humans (as opposed to animals and other forms of nature). Some think that this group has a basis in humanity, in that some of our DNA comes from their race, meaning that they were here prior to us in the distant past.

When you hear of Pleiadeans, you usually also hear about a great Council and other species of the universe, i.e., the Acturians. (I do need to add that within the past month, I've heard some negative things about this group—a first. But I pass that to you as well.)

ACTURIANS

One group seems to move easily into the other as one researches alien temperaments. This group was first mentioned (as far as I know, and I *could* be wrong) by Edgar Casey. Now, everyone knows his success rate. He said that this group would one day contact us from the star Arturus in the Bootes constellation and that they were a benevolent race. These healing individuals are smaller than the typical human, usually about three to four feet tall. With a turquoise-like skin color, they have large oval eyes, three fingers on two hands, and communicate mostly via telepathy. They live for hundreds of years.

REPTILIANS

I choose to list this grouping as an example, but this will be a species that we will not be using for this process. They seem to be uniformly connected to government conspiracy theories and great manipulation of our planet. From most sources, these are the "bad guys" of the galaxy, hailing from the Draco constellation, and they've scattered themselves everywhere, trying to insert evil wherever they go. (Again, this is all hearsay because no one I've met has actually seen or interacted with one.) They are also called Lizard People, Reptoids, and Reptilian Aliens. Unfortunately, there have been reports that this group can disguise their members as humans with thin, fit bodies at about six to nine feet tall. Others say that they are more visually like…well like you've seen in the movies and on television: snake eyes, clawed hands and feet, and bigger than any reptile should be. Let's not dig deeper here. We will stay away, just in case.

MANTIS

The Mantis group has been sourced as being both bad and good, and I'd say that most stories are either really bad or wonderfully good. I personally have seen two in my meditations and contactee experiences and can say that I've seen the good ones. They are said to be highly intelligent and very much telepathic individuals. The Mantis are often suspected to be supervisors in abduction scenarios. They have very large eyes of the insect variety, yellow-green skin, and they are very tall. Though some have said only five to six feet in height, I've also heard of those that have had to duck way down when coming through doors, which would indicate well over seven to nine feet. And…they look like the insect we call the praying mantis. That might scare the socks off you at first, but I think that they deserve consideration (the good ones, that is).

MEN IN BLACK

Typically dressed as their name implies, this group could be part of the government conspiracy group, so we will not be looking for their help in this methodology, just in case. Some say they are actual human government "employees" out to scare the would-be UFO sighter into being very quiet about their alien experiences. Just keep your real eyes peeled for the classic dark, perfectly maintained vehicles (though of late I've heard reports of them driving other vehicles—jeeps), pale-skinned men with what I call birth-control sun glasses (thick dark-rimmed). (They will not look like Tommy Lee Jones or Will Smith. At least I don't think so...)

BIGFOOT, SASQUATCH, THE ABOMINABLE SNOWMAN, ETC.

Who knows? Alien or misunderstood woodland creature. We won't be calling on these guys either; again, just to be safe.

WATER BABIES, BIRDS, INSECTS

These lifeforms are unlikely to be part of your process here, but in case you do have need of them or happen to see one, you will find water creatures that are, according to Nancy Leider:

...crablike, fishlike, squidlike, or formed like almost any of your ocean inhabitants—an almost infinite variety.

You may also see strange birds and it helps to know that there are a huge number of insects (that I don't see you interacting with, but if you do, please don't tell me—shivering here).

The whole idea of knowing these varied types is that one or more of them will be popping up to help you with your alien and UFO management. You will interact with them. They will try to assist you. They are not going to frighten or manipulate you. They will become teachers and givers of information that you have stored, just waiting for the age of disclosure.

OTHER DIMENSIONAL CREATURES/BEINGS?

I was ready to say that this section was complete with some of the main varieties of entities that you might encounter. Then during one very recent experience, well after this book had been written, I was greeted by something (someone) new—someone who I'd put in an entirely different category. Thinking about it more, I did realize that there was truth to the idea that those in other dimensions were certainly alien, but this one? Hmmm.

FAIRY FOLK

As I proceeded through my process, I was met with a fairy. He was about a foot tall, beige-to-brown in color and had big pointed ears. He immediately brought to mind author and artist Beth Wilder's vision of *A Tarot of Faery*. I'd been exposed to the "myths" and stories of this group for many years and had fallen in love with fairy houses, fairy doors, fairy tales, and more at varied times, but was told early on in meditation with the Light Beings that fairies (who *were* real they said) required much work to establish and keep a relationship—they were terribly high maintenance and things could go badly if one was not diligent. "You have enough on your plate, without inviting fairy folk into your life," they'd said.

The fairy I met in this particular process said that he was a Veda. Not recognizing the title, I went immediately to the Internet to see if anyone else was aware of this fairy group. I, of course, came right away to the Vedic religion of India and did recall that there were those I knew who practiced this ancient belief system. It would seem that according to Hindu "vedas" (which are scriptures), there are 4,000 species of humans and subhumans (and these included aliens). Further research showed me that there seemed to be an entire "colony" of imagery of artistic persuasion showing Veda Fairies—real? Haven't a clue. There's much written about Veda involving fairy tales. Did I spell "Veda" wrong? Was it "Vida" instead? If so, even Walt Disney was part of the culture. So, was this individual I met a Veda fairy? Or was he just telling me to research the Vedic principles? I offer a shrug and a promise of more research.

Tales about fairies have been know to spawn from some tidbits of reality, like folklore. I'm no stranger, too, to the fairies that infiltrate the world of paranormal research. I've had many authors who have caught such creatures on film. (I don't plan to go into the history of them here as researched in Stuart Schnieder's *Ghost in the Cemetery* series, but there is much written about them.) Beth Wilder has had up-close and personal contact with fairies, which inspired her to write and illustrate her popular Tarot deck. It appeared that a massive amount of research needed to be conducted.

But back to my experience. The fairy I met in the process wondered why their group of other dimensional beings were not featured in this book, because they most certainly were going to be participating for some of those who use it. ***Okay,*** I thought. So, though, I'm certainly not versed in this group, I offer that fairies or similar creatures may show up for you. Be cognizant of them and remember it is your decision whether you decide to work with them or not.

MOVING ON...

As I work on this process and find my own conclusions, I would be remiss not to mention that my experience of positivity will not be reflected for everyone. In fact, there is an entire faction of UFO researchers who have a completely different view of star beings. In fairness to looking at both sides of a coin, some find that alien interaction is not only bad, but extremely dangerous. Jordan Hofer, author of *Evolutionary Ufology,* MUFON Research Specialist in Anthropology, and an author for the UFO phenomena has this to say about alien exposures:

Much has been reported about friendly aliens helping humanity, but where is the evidence for this? Have they cured a single disease? Offered one piece of advanced technology? Given us any source of alternative energy? Suggested some solution to our environmental problems? Saved even one child from starvation? No, no, no, no, and no! If the Reptilians and Mantids do in fact exist, they care as little for us as do the Grays. They are not our friends and they are not here to help.

That goes for every other reported space brother. None of them holds any empathy for us. Apparently, all spacefaring species that have come to Earth are emotionally retarded.

If Hofer's research is correct, then great care must be exercised when using this process. He further mentions in *Evolutionary Ufology* that the "grays" are compulsive liars. So where does this leave us? Hofer does not say that these entities do not exist. He tells us to be careful, least we become victims. This makes the protections of ourselves and our livelihood of supreme importance.

I would make the suggestion here, that if you've had a bad abduction experience, you may wish to contact a reputable hypnotherapist in your area and allow a professional to work with you first before using these methods. Calling these things up, could be hazardous. I've had all good experiences, as I've mentioned, but if you have not had that luxury, it may be time to say *no* to further enticements here for the time being.

THE MIND/BODY/SPIRIT APPROACH YOUR PERSONAL PROTECTION

Before we move into the mechanics of alien and UFO management, a very important piece must be learned and utilized: personal protection. Many who are reading this book will say: I ground myself. I put up personal protection. My [God, angels, deity, goddess, etc.] protects me. I pray every day.

I say that this is wonderful thing that you may have a protection practice in place. I come to you with a warning now.

There needs to be additional protection from some important, powerful source before
—I REPEAT, *BEFORE*—
you begin this process.

What, you may ask, do I do about this if I don't believe in God? Believing in, or not believing, in God (or UFOs and aliens) has nothing to do with what is and what isn't. You still must have further protection. The best thing to do here then is to appeal to the universe for additional defenses.

WHAT CAN GO WRONG IF YOU DON'T HAVE PROTECTION?

Your life can be drastically changed for the worse if you don't have the appropriate protection because you really don't know what or who you are summoning to interact with you. You have to have a "gatekeeper" to make sure that nothing of a questionable nature gets through to your mind or body or daily life. It's much like the Ouija Board or pendulums/ dowsing rods. You can just as easily have an evil entity pop into your life that you can't control as to have a benign individual. Having personal protection designed specifically for you, by you, is imperative.

If you are at this point in the text and are thinking: *I don't need more protection. I already invoke a higher power. I don't want to read this part. I'll skip this for now. I don't think it's necessary*...If you are in any way deciding *not* to protect yourself in this additional manner, I ask that you put this book down. Yes, it's that important. Don't read another sentence. Put it back on the book shelf. You're better off not knowing any of this.

I'm hoping, however, that you are taking this seriously and wish to continue. To begin this process, feel free to use your own "prayer" or words to protect yourself. But you must add a supplementary section to this calling in of protection. You will need additional protection specifically aimed toward these sessions that cover every space around you.

A PRAYER TO MICHAEL

I learned of this extra protection need after I began to learn animal communications. There was a prayer offered during that process as well and I routinely used one and was protected by an animal who was willing to take on that kind of thing for me. For me, it was a horse I'd met (in my mind because that's where animal communications take place for me) by the name of Solo. He was a horse belonging to another student in an animal communications class I was taking taught by Anita Curtis in Pennsylvania (http://anitacurtis.com). Solo is with me to this day, overlooking any animal communication session I become involved with.

It was sometime after Solo came to be with me that I went to an Angel Workshop taught by Pat Cassel in Pennsylvania (www.angelhealer555.com). She channels angels. I remember her standing in front of me and looking confused.

"What do you do for a living?" she asked.

"I'm an editor," I answered.

She squinted and looked even more confused, "Why am I sensing ghosts…and other strange things?"

"Well," I said, "I am an editor for a paranormal line of books—ghosts, UFOs, that kind of thing."

She was nodding now. "Yes, now I understand. Archangel Michael says you do not have enough protection for what you do. Very dangerous sometimes..."

I, of course, told her that I had plenty of protection. (I had Solo, I said my prayers to God, I grounded myself on ghost investigations. Basically, I thought I had it all covered. Apparently, not so much.)

She said, "You need much more for your line of work. You must be covered every minute by the Archangels if you are working with the otherside—or *any* side."

Hmmmm. After class, she gave me a prayer that I immediately put into play. I uttered it each morning at my computer as I began working with the paranormal authors, their books, and other strange issues of the day. I used it within myself in addition to the group meditations held at paranormal investigations, I said it before going into any hypnotic or visualization experience involving UFOs or aliens, and I said it to keep experiences out of my bedroom at night. (Ghosts, and aliens, etc., love that popping in at the bottom of the bed stuff and I just can't deal with that...)

The point that I want to make after telling you this is that my life improved immediately. I mean *immediately.* I felt better physically, mentally, and spiritually. It was as though a weight had been lifted. Apparently, I'd been under... well, attack—not exactly *attack* I suppose, because most of what I'd dealt with at that time was of a benign nature, but there were many spirits weighing in, even though I'd not recognized it.

You must be cognizant of the need of extra protection. It is ***NOT* OPTIONAL**.

The prayer I learned from Pat Cassel's angel workshop has been incorporated into my protection prayer whenever I deal with the paranormal, any mind/body/spirit topic, and UFO/alien research. I always take the time to say it. It doesn't matter who is waiting on me, I say the prayer (with a bit of my own variation). It is as follows:

May the love of God be with me and in me.
And fill me with the white love of love and protection.
I come to you in Christ Consciousness.
Come to me in Christ Consciousness.

I ask for the full protection of Lord Michael, the Archangel of protection.
Lord Michael in front,

Lord Michael behind,
Lord Michael to the right,
Lord Michael to the left,
Lord Michael above,
Lord Michael below,
Lord Michael, Lord Michael wherever I go.

I am His love protecting here.
I am His love protecting here.
I am His love protecting here.

If you are a believer in angels or God, feel free to use this prayer. It does its job.

Note that the two lines about Christ Consciousness do not necessarily mean Jesus Christ as the Savior in the Christian religion, but rather his *mind*, which is of the highest good. So this is not a religious line of thought specifically (unless you want it to be); it merely aligns you with the highest element of good that can be reached for you.

If you do not believe in angels or God, you can replace the angelic protection, making your prayer to your deity of choice or to the universe. It does not matter as long as the *highest power* that *is* protects you. This prayer can be manipulated to help you with your personal reign of being. It needs to be said that research should be done on the name you decide to use to make sure that protection is part of his/her/its arsenal. For example, though St. Francis is a wonderful saint for animals, he may not necessarily be the best choice for your overall protection for UFO research.

To include another protective being, you might say instead:

May the love of [God, or any religious figure or Saint, or the universe] be with me and in me.

And fill me with the white love of love and protection.

I come to you in Christ [God, or any religious figure or Saint, or the universe] Consciousness.

Come to me in Christ [God, or any religious figure or Saint, or the universe] Consciousness.

I ask for the full protection of Lord Michael, the Archangel of protection [God, or any religious figure or Saint, or the universe].

[Name of protector] in front,
[Name of protector] behind,
[Name of protector] to the right,
[Name of protector] to the left,
[Name of protector] above,
[Name of protector] below,
[Name of protector], [name of protector] wherever I go.

I am [his, her, its] love protecting here.
I am [his, her, its] love protecting here.
I am [his her, its] love protecting here.

This should be uttered either out loud or internally before any movement towards alien and UFO research, and especially at all times *prior to* using the methods discussed here.

RELAXATION, INTERPRETATION, & A BEAST OF BURDEN

SOME PRELIMINARIES

Once you have protected yourself with the prayer that fits your beliefs and being, there are other things to think about prior to working with aliens and UFOs. There is a visualization precursor that is very symbolic of the things you will be going through. Each portion of the "buildup" is not only important individually, but also as a collective. Visualization is much easier (for most people) than actual meditation, though, if you are relaxed enough, it can lead into meditation. For our purposes, we will be using an in-depth visualization to introduce you to one of the major players as you look to finding out about any alien/UFO experience that needs to be brought to the surface and cataloged.

In hypnosis, this portion is the relaxation phase, which relaxes your body and mind. You do not lose consciousness or awareness at any time during the entire process. This part puts you in an alpha state to prepare your psyche. In this exercise, however, it is more about relaxation than preparation. As you move through this process, you will need a "Beast of Burden" to take some of the weight from your shoulders. This weight will be different for every person, but may include the following:

- Fear of what's to come
- Uncertainty regarding your abilities
- Items to be carried
- Discussion with someone who understands you intimately

- Comic relief
- Reality checks
- Weariness
- Remembrances

There are many others, depending on your specific and very individual needs. You may find that in the first few practices, you may not need assistance at all from a source outside yourself. At a later time, it may come in handy. It would be wise, then, to have it along all the time, just in case.

You are wondering, of course, what this beast may look like. In other forms of visualization, such an entity would be developed by the person involved with the method. You would develop and visualize your own helper. (This is not to say that you can't do that here if you so wish, but it does take some of your concentration away from the experience until it becomes second nature. That is a personal choice.) This will not be the case here, for time spent will be needed for the actual alien interaction and should not be taxed with discovering helpers. We will, therefore, be using a specific beast to orient you to the progress.

ENTER: THE CAMEL

I'm sure that most know what kind of an animal the camel is and have usually seen one, if only in a zoo or on nature television programs. Specifics about the camel are not really that important. It's good to know that it can be about seven feet tall and carry up to 200 pounds. Two breeds (the Dromedary (one-hump) and the Bactrian (two-humps) are closely related in temperament. For the most part, and for our purposes, the camel is domesticated and a likely companion for your journey. They spit when provoked (not saliva as many think, but undigested food). They have excellent sight and smell. They are quiet on their feet and can weigh up to 1,500 pounds.

As you begin your exercise, the camel will already be there waiting for you. It does not matter that it is not a resident of your area normally (unless in Asia, North Africa, the Middle East, etc.). He or she will "have your back" throughout, providing you any number of services should you need them. Sometimes your camel will be quiet as a mouse—services not needed. Other times, he or she may be quite adamant and involved. It just depends on the scenario.

I again am asking that you suspend belief and drop yourself into a fantasy world. This camel will have a personality that you will impose upon it. It will be your companion and provide you with emotional sustenance, it will walk with you, carry any burden you feel you will need for your journey, and will materialize anything you need out of thin air.

When you first begin this process, the personality of the camel may be murky because you've not worked in this manner before. As you continue in the months that follow, you will find that your camel will become a good friend. He or she may even give you a name to call him/her by. You may wish to do further research on the species to understand it more fully, since it will have full knowledge of you. (Lately, those working through their process with me have been finding that the camel interacting with them has had the name Mike. This because of a car insurance television commercial where the camel talks to worker Mike. It's interesting how many people have said this to me. They don't necessarily remember the advertised product, but they remember the camel.)

In the interim, just a bit of knowledge of the camel's customary behaviors will be appropriate.

Now that you understand your partner in this exercise, you will need to produce a list of questions that you might like answered during your sessions. There may be some of you who do not think or do not remember ever having had a UFO or alien experience. These questions will reflect that. Others will remember one or more experiences, but there will be gaps in memory. Still others will have great details and will merely want confirmation. The final group will just want a recording mechanism to begin a detailed entry of their times with the varied alien populace. Note these questions as only the beginning. You may have many more. Or, once you begin to use this process and have maintained several visitations, the questions will become more direct, detailed, or focused on independent variables. This list can be exhaustive for you. Some will be answered, others will be strived to be answered at some future point. Some questions may relate directly to you, others may link to others about you, including the world and outward-looking questions.

Note that in the Appendix, you will have various pages showing these questions, making it easy to refer back to them.

QUESTIONS FOR THOSE WHO BELIEVE THEY HAVE HAD AN EXPERIENCE

1. What are the particulars of the experience: date, time, place?
2. What feelings do I remember having before the experience?
3. What happened during the experience? (Other questions may arise as this description moves forward.)
4. Do I remember the craft and descriptions of the beings present? (Note details.)
5. Do I remember how the incident ended?
6. How did I feel after the event? The next day?
7. Are there ongoing dreams or new encounters related to this one?
8. Have I discussed the situation with someone who understands?
9. Did I learn anything from this encounter? (About myself, about the beings, about the Earth or Universe?)
10. Should I report the incident?

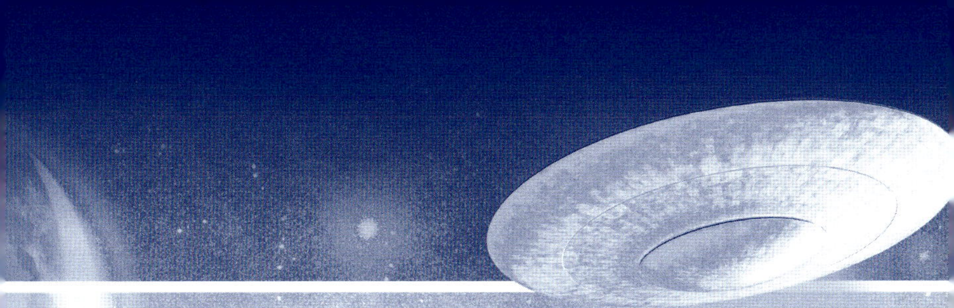

QUESTIONS FOR THOSE WHO DO NOT BELIEVE THEY HAVE HAD AN EXPERIENCE

1. Have I ever had an experience involving a UFO or alien?
2. Have I ever had another reincarnated life in which I've had a UFO or alien experience?
3. Am I blocking alien experiences? If so, how? If so, why?
4. If I've had an experience, when did the first one occur?
5. Where did it occur?
6. What were the specifics?
7. Are there gaps or screens of memory that I'm not aware of? What do they entail?
8. Did I learn something from the experience?
9. Was I harmed during the experience?
10. Why was I chosen for the experience?
11. Was the UFO/alien satisfied with the results of the experience?
12. Were/are there others within my family who have also had this experience, specifically related to my personal experience? What are the particulars?

QUESTIONS FOR SOMEONE WHO REMEMBERS AN EXPERIENCE(S), BUT FINDS GAPS IN THEIR MEMORIES

1. When did the first experience occur?

2. Where did it occur?

3. What were the specifics?

4. What are the gaps or screens of memory that I'm not aware of? What do they entail?

5. Did I learn something from the experience?

6. Was I harmed during the experience?

7. Why was I chosen for the experience?

8. Was the UFO/alien satisfied with the results of the experience?

9. Were/are there others within my family who have also had this experience, specifically related to my personal experience? What are the specifics?

QUESTIONS FOR THOSE WISHING TO CONFIRM THE DETAILS OF AN EXPERIENCE

(Similar to the questions for those who believe they've had an experience, but more detailed and usually used at a later time.)

1. When did the first experience occur?
2. Where did it occur?
3. What were the specifics?
4. Are there gaps or screens of memory that I'm not aware of? What do they entail?
5. What did I learn from the experience?
6. Was I harmed during the experience?
7. Why was I chosen for the experience?
8. Was the UFO/alien satisfied with the results of the experience? What did they learn?
9. Were/are there others within my family who have also had this experience, specifically related to my personal experience? What are the specifics?

PREPARING FOR VISUALIZATION

The following will be a visualization that will relax you, bringing you to the beginning of your management program. This particular part of the system sometimes becomes problematic for people. Those who do not routinely meditate or practice some kind of internal ritual may find it difficult to suspend the thoughts of their daily lives long enough to make visualization successful. Unfortunately, this section is not optional, so a way around this must be explored if this describes you.

Oftentimes, people who cannot enter into a relaxed state by themselves *can* when working with another person. Too, even if one does meditate, it sometimes works better operating in pairs. When working with another, we call this guided visualization. Someone else will read the section to you as you picture the scene described in your mind. There will be dialog between the two of you as you move through the process (whereas if alone, the dialog is usually internal, or if speaking out loud, recorded for later listening).

The best suggestion is to read through this entire book, especially the process section, before starting, and then decide whether you would benefit from working in a grouping of two or more, or working alone. Both are acceptable. You may wish to try it alone at first, and if the results are not to your liking, then choose a partner. Obviously, this partner should be like-minded.

There are several methods of tracking your experiences. Management of this is nearly as important as the experience itself, because it will be your jumping-off point for deeper research or new experiences. Recording sessions on any type of audio device is suggested. It need not be an impressive contraption. Old cassette recorders, mini recorders, computer recorders, digital recorders—all of them will be appropriate. You are not in need of expensive equipment. We will not be looking for EVP (Electronic Voice Phenomena), though it should not surprise you if you do obtain some amazing EVP anyway. The idea is to have reference for any material that you might forget, do not understand, or for transcription. You will find that although you feel as though you've been "under" for just a few minutes, sometimes the likelihood is that your view of time is incorrect and you've been going through your experience for an hour or longer (an excellent example of time concepts and why understanding time is important). Recording is the only real way to know that, however, unless you are working in pairs or keep a timepiece close by.

Transcription would be ideal, meaning that you would transcribe from the recorder to a print media for later reflection. It is appropriate, if you choose, to have a partner or someone to take notes when the session is underway; however, much data is lost during this method. It is difficult to write all that will come to light without missing vital information. I do know that some begin without recording until they see exactly what will happen. Then at a later time, they note their experiences. Some information is lost this way, but due to human nature, I know that this will occur, so just try to get the notes down in some form as quickly as you can, after the session, to prevent memory loss if you are not using recording equipment. I will warn you here again that memory loss of a session is of high occurrence, especially if working alone. (You can always choose to revisit the experience at another time, though.)

There will be forms in the Appendix that you can use to model your progress of the five parts of this management process into:

- Relaxation
- The Climb to Management
- Management Interaction
- The Way Back
- Processing

RELAXATION

Before you begin the relaxation process, find yourself a comfortable, quiet place. The chair you sit in should be comfortable, but not too comfortable. You don't want to fall asleep. This too is why you should not lie down, unless you are working with a partner who can monitor whether you fall asleep or not.

Things that interfere with this quiet place should be controlled. No telephones, no barking dogs or lap cats, no outside noises, no child-related (or any person for that matter) interruptions. To help with sending the outside world away, it may be a good idea to have white noise available, such as that found with varied clocks or relaxation equipment. These tools can be set usually to simulate rain, an evening forest (with crickets, etc.), ocean waves, and several other sounds. Using such a method can drown out the normalcy around you. (This, however, is optional.)

Taking some of the light from the room is also helpful, though not necessary. Dim lighting often is in itself an invitation to relaxation.

Water to drink should be available in case you need it, though it most likely won't be consumed until after the session. You may feel very thirsty at that point. Water will help ground you into the present once the session is over.

If you choose to have a partner, that person should have this script available, as well as the questions lists, and make sure that even in low light, there is enough light to read by or to take notes. That person should also have water available because there may be times during the process where the voice will become "crackly." Water should be taken in between sentences or parts, allowing the person undergoing the process a "soft" time to relax without voice. Make sure a partner has time to read over the script prior to working with you, or at the very least before the session. Though stumbling over words is not a huge issue, it can be a distraction to your process, because remember, you will be aware of all that goes on and will definitely hear a mistake. Your brain will attack it, taking away your concentration.

The script must be delivered very slowly if a partner is reading it. There must be time for you to visualize the scenes provided. If you are working alone, you will need to commit some of the script and its scenery to memory so that you can take yourself through the steps in a slow fashion. This script need not be memorized word-for-word. Knowing the concept will allow you to work through the management process in your own way with your own interpretation of a relaxing scene. The script will be written as though you are saying the words to yourself, for yourself. If you have a partner working with you, the "I" should be replaced by "you," etc. Note that if you do not feel relaxed enough by going down 10 steps (see the following script), this can be increased to 20 steps—or more if needed. Be aware that the further you are relaxed, the possibility of falling asleep increases.

TIP: *If you are someone who relaxes quickly and easily, use the script as written. If you need more time to relax, increase the number of steps that go down into the valley from 10 to 20 (even more if you need them). During those extra steps, you should be concentrating on your breathing and looking out over the valley as you descend, seeing the foliage, the trees, etc. The goal is relaxation, so don't cut it short if you need more.*

The relaxation script is as follows:

I will start with my breathing, because my breathing will keep me calm and relaxed throughout my session. To begin, I will take a deep breath in and hold it for three counts—one, two, three—and release it slowly. Now I will tighten all the muscles in my body, then release and relax my muscles. Again, I will tighten all the muscles in my body, then release and relax my muscles. I will take another breath in—one, two, three—and release it. One more time, a breath in—one, two, three—and release.

I will now imagine a bright white light. I see it in the distance moving toward me and I know that this is a healing light, a relaxing light, a protecting light. I see it moving closer to me… and still closer. It is now right in front of me and I notice that there is not only white light, but there are green and yellow swirls of energy going through it. This light will keep me safe as I move into my mind and my experience. It will keep me safe, comfortable, and relaxed. It will never leave me. I will be able to observe everything I intend to look at without fear or worry, because this light will soothe me and keep me safe, and comfortable, and relaxed. This light now moves to me and surrounds me in its pure warm safety. It engulfs me and I soak it in because I know that it will keep me safe, comfortable, and protected, no matter what. It fills my whole body and I can see a glow as I look down at my arms and legs. I see it and feel it.

The only entities that will be able to enter my field of light are those for my highest good. I may interact with my higher self, the masters and guides, and highly evolved loving entities. Any star being that I encounter must respect this white light and come no closer unless allowed by my higher self, my guides, or God. In this way, only those with my highest good can actually touch me. Others may speak to me, but no one can harm me, nothing can upset me because I am only observing at this time. I am totally protected by this pure light.

Now that I have my protective light within me, I notice 10 steps going down to a green and flower-covered valley. I will go down these steps very slowly. Every step downward, I will become ten times more relaxed than I am right now.

One: *I am so relaxed.*

Two: *I breathe in and out slowly.*

Three: *I look down as I move down the steps and see all the beautiful flowers at the bottom of the stairs.*

Four: *The flowers are all the colors of the rainbow and more.*

Five: *I see green, and blue, and purple, and pink, and yellow.*

Six: *The flowers bloom from a vast green meadow.*

Seven: *I breathe in and out slowly.*

Eight: *I am more relaxed than I've ever been.*

Nine: *Relaxed, comfortable, protected.*

Ten: *I am standing on a path with beautiful flowers all around me.*

THE CLIMB TO MANAGEMENT

(There should be some time given, so that the flowers and scenery are enjoyed—about two minutes of quiet should suffice.)

I am standing on the beautiful pathway in the valley and notice that a camel stands to one side. He welcomes me and makes me feel relaxed and safe. He is there to accompany me on my journey. He speaks with me…

(Leave about one minute for the camel to talk. He may speak his name and tell you how he will help you, he may tell you about things he is carrying, he may invite you to ride him, or he may just encourage you in some way.)

The two of us begin our journey by following the flowered pathway. We look at all the colorful flora and we can smell their sweet fragrances. I put my hand on the camel's neck and feel his soft fur. I feel so safe and comfortable and protected with him near. Soon, we see that the pathway is moving upward, climbing the side of the mountain toward the blue sky. The climb is not steep, but goes steadily up. My camel and I are totally relaxed and move up the pathway easily. We notice the trees and shrubbery to the sides of the path—so lush and green. I reach out and touch the rounded leaves of a bush and listen to the buzzing of the insects that comes from within the forest landscape. The sounds are relaxing and I walk forward and upward, enjoying the company of my camel.

(Leave about one minute for the camel to interact.)

We are getting closer to the top of the path that will put us on top the mountain. I can see the puffy clouds in the blue sky and feel the warm sunshine on my face as I climb the path.

I am only a few steps away from reaching the top of the path and will be able to stand on the mountain top, with the clouds and the beautiful sky. I feel my heartbeat speed up just a bit, because I know that there will be someone on top the mountain who will guide me through my first journey. Who will it be? Where will I go?

The camel is moving ahead of me and I'm following him closer and closer to the top. The camel is now disappearing over the top edge of the path onto the mountain top. I am following close behind.

I now see who will be there helping me.

(Leave time for identification of the entity there to help you and a description.)

MANAGEMENT INTERACTION

This is where the lists of questions are used, depending on who or what you see as you cross over the mountain top. These lists should be handy if a partner is working with you. If you are working alone, you should have in memory most of the questions. More will come to light as you talk with the individual who will be leading you through the process, be it guide or alien. You may find, though, that your experience does not require questions. You will be able to judge this during your experience. Use these questions as a jumping-off point, in case you find yourself at a standstill. (See the sample from an actual case management session in the Appendix.)

At the top of the mountain, in addition to the guide who will be with you to help you to understand the UFO or star being experience, the Light Beings will be there to assist and observe, consisting of five tubes of light that encompass universal composure. These being will be observers and givers of advice throughout, if needed, or if you need to call upon them for any reason. They will have the knowledge of raising vibrations for you and yours. They say the following about the arrival at the top of the mountain:

> Your vibration becomes very important for future endeavors. If you do not go into this visualization process in the right frame of mind, a lower vibration might occur. This would prevent you from moving ahead in your human life on Earth to complete your lessons. The best example of this can be gleaned if you find that you are focused on the "me" as opposed to the learning of the outward universe. Though you may find that, surely, some of your experience will be dedicated to you alone (for this is how we connect with you), there will be a learning curve as well that takes into consideration many factors for humanity outside the self.
>
> Management does not come lightly. It may take several visits to the mountain reflecting a lone experience before the entire lesson is both known and accepted. You must understand that these lessons and experiences have a specific purpose for the universal connections that you will need to make in the near future. You will want to stay on the right side of God and not stray to the self motivations that cause others pain or difficulty. You may be saying now that this is difficult to do since the process here is so new and reflections on oneself is really the reason you've picked up this book. We as the Light Beings understand this. These things are taken into consideration, but if you find that, on the average, these management lessons and retrievals are focused primarily on you and not on helping others, this should be quickly addressed. This is where your guide, your camel, and we, the Light Beings, can be summoned to put you on the right track. We will be observing just as you and will maintain a distance so as not to interfere in your encounter. However, during this time, your questions about your own life and your own experience, once answered, should then allow you to move on to discuss the larger picture.

Following are sample questions for the universe, but there may be others that you have in mind.

QUESTIONS FOR THE UNIVERSE

- How do I fit into the big picture?
- Have I learned all I need to learn from this experience?
- How does this experience move humanity forward?
- Why am I here?
- Who needs my help?

THE WAY BACK

This part of the visualization process will advise your guide and anyone involved with your experience that you wish to leave and return to full consciousness and into your current life.

I will now be returning to my life, leaving behind any individuals and experiences. However, I will remember each part of my story or experience with perfect clarity.

I am beginning to come back to myself. I tighten and then relax my muscles. I open my eyes and take in a deep breath. I'm back.

RECORDING AND RESEARCHING YOUR EXPERIENCES

THE IMPORTANCE OF GETTING IT AS EXACT AS YOU CAN

The importance of putting your experience down on paper or into a computer file as soon as you are finished with the visualization cannot be stressed enough. Oddly, and as mentioned prior, in UFO and alien abduction/contactee experiences, forgetting the details happens more often than not. If you don't record the experience right away, the only way you will remember all the details is when (or if) the thought is triggered in some fashion. Triggers are different for every person and from session to session. It is practically impossible to predict a trigger. Author and investigator Rev. Debra Marshall advises that smells and sounds can be powerful triggers for some. You, of course, could revisit any experience, simply by advising the camel prior to your visualization script or the guide who arrives to assist. But this does not, unfortunately, guarantee that the details will be revealed again.

FORM

A form that is located in the Appendix is merely a "cheat sheet." You can use a journal or a larger sheet than the 6" x 9" paper shown in this book. Items on the form can be changed to fit your personal brand of management. The form is for your convenience, should you prefer something more specific. It can be adapted for your usage.

SHOULD YOU REPORT YOUR EXPERIENCE? WHAT'S THE VALUE?

Reporting your experiences is a personal choice. It helps to remember that these kinds of experiences are so personal and so subjective that a true agency researching UFOs may not accept your words as proof and there is ridicule around the planet for this kind of thing. Now becomes the time when you know in your heart that what you've experienced during this process is indeed true for you. As I mentioned earlier, I often tell people who are skeptical: Once it happens to you, then you know it's true and real. And who cares what someone else thinks?

Therefore, I remind you that you do not have to prove something to anyone. The main crux of this endeavor is to find out the secrets that have been screened or hidden within your own mind, and then what to do with that information. You may need it for healing purposes or you may just want to know what has happened, feeling that no one has the right to keep that from you. Rarely does anyone travel down this road for the purpose of reporting it to someone else. While it's true that some investigators will accept your experience as fact, those who do not, tend to "rock the boat" of your mind. You begin to question yourself and your experience. That is not healthy. Do not allow others to judge you.

A barometer that I use has been brought down to a single question: Does the reporting of my experience help someone else? If it helps someone, reporting is a good thing. If not, or if the assistance to someone else is negligible, it may be better to keep your own records for yourself only. Who needs the drama?

INSTIGATING AN EXPERIENCE

Through conducting your research, some of you may find that you have not had an experience, and might like to have one. Please know that if you go down *this* road, inviting an experience, there may be pitfalls. You have little control over what/who will come, or when. To this point in this book, the contact has already been made and our process has been to relive/research those instances, bringing to light something that you may not have known prior to. Calling down a UFO or alien is a whole different animal and should not be considered lightly.

WHAT COULD GO WRONG?

Trust me when I say that things could go wrong. Or...maybe they won't. We just don't know and have no way to gauge what could happen if successful. To instigate an experience (commonly called a contactee experience), you first must do the research. Understand the field of ufology. Read, read, read. But don't just read books that regurgitate varied sightings. Read about people who have had actual experiences (for example, *Alien Encounters in the Western United States* by Tracie Austin). Talk to people who channel biblical figures and saints. Does this take time? Yes. Is it worth the wait to make the call? Well, let me offer this: Suppose you make the call and a UFO not only comes out from the clouds or up from the seas, but it just so happens to be a Reptilian ship and does not have your welfare at its center. You never want to have to say: *I wish I'd never done that.* It would be too late (especially if you've been hurt because of it). Is that harsh? I haven't a clue. Just know what you're doing. What I've given you here is very sparse as far as the knowledge you should have prior to going in cold.

A method of calling a UFO for an experience can be explored in Gerard Medvec's book, *Mid-Atlantic UFOs,* under the story "The Nine." The people in the story—nine individuals in New York—have had a 100 percent success rate at calling down a UFO. Jordan Hofer's book, *Evolutionary Ufology* will give you all the reasons why this might not be a good idea. Research and read both sides of the issue.

I personally have had success calling down a UFO in a positive fashion using the protection methods and relaxation methods shown here. I, along with author/researcher Gerry Medvec and researcher Vicki Stong, saw nineteen (19!) UFOs visit using techniques related by "The Nine," which included ten days of meditation on the visitation, before stationing ourselves in an area where UFO activity had been reported prior.

WHAT WON'T YOU ALLOW?

Having made all those frightening points, let me say that I have had success in dictating the circumstances regarding what I don't want when dealing with both UFO/Alien experiences or those of the paranormal variety.

I, of course, use the protection prayer for "me and mine" every night before bed, so I know the protection is there. But I've also, during my paranormal days, said out loud in my home that I don't want anything happening to me while I'm asleep. Too many regressions have shown me that alien or ghost figures popping up at the bottom of one's bed is a constant. And I don't like that. I don't want that. I want to be fully engaged with my brain before having any kind of experience. I can tell you that I've not had trouble like that for over seven years (that I know of). So is it the protective prayer? The Light Beings that I channel watching over me? God? Or do aliens really hate barking ankle biters? (A joke of course. The late author Lee Prosser often told me how the Greys would visit and put out calming vibes for his cats who always alerted him when someone was around. Yet I have also heard that the Greys are the universe's trouble makers. Questions remain...)

I've actually, via channeling the Light Beings, been asked if a Zeta could visit me inside a dream to discuss some very negative press that group was getting from an online radio broadcast. Looking back, it's a funny story. I'd given permission because I wanted answers. I went to go to bed, lights out, husband already sleeping...I lay my head down on the pillow and I began to hear knocking on the walls. I screamed out in my mind: "No, no! I said *after* I was asleep! I don't want to see you here!" After saying that, I remembered nothing until the next morning. I was put out that fast. And the next morning, I felt great. There were none of the fears about what I'd heard the radio show host discuss. I felt peace. *However*, I had no information regarding what happened during that "visit." Have there been other clandestine visits? (This is on my list to research further with this process.)

All that to say again that it would *seem* that they will respect your boundaries. Well...maybe. I just don't know. Others will say not. They could be right as well. Parameters are unclear.

I've come back to this spot months after writing the prior words because I've found a glitch in my own armor and therefore one that could be passed on inadvertently to you. At work, while editing the book *A Silent Invasion: The Truth About Aliens, Alien Abductions, and UFOs* by Rev. Debra Marshall, something happened that I'd not expected.

First, let me say that I've never had bad dreams or nightmares—I just never have them. One night, after one of my classic cluster headaches, I went into my living room in the middle of the night to try to sleep in a recliner so as not to disturb my husband. Once settled and in a light sleep, very suddenly, I started to have some kind of bad dream (I don't remember it) and I had what I can describe as an almost out-of-body feeling like my soul was being pulled out of my body. My mind was screaming abduction. At that exact moment my little dog (with a serious big yapping mouth) started barking furiously. He wasn't in bed as usual; he was with me in the living room. I woke startled, with my heart pounding out of my chest and screaming out in my head my protection prayer to Archangel Michael. At that moment also, my husband got up and came out from the bedroom to ask me if I was okay. He'd had a bad dream too that he couldn't remember and was startled awake thinking of me. It was the first time I'd been frightened upon waking in my own home, and I knew that it was different than other nights. Something had nearly happened to me—I was sure of it.

Then the very next night, I was in bed and it was around 12:30 a.m. or so and I was having a regular stupid dream (again I don't remember it except to say that it was typical) and I suddenly had the feeling that there was an unwelcome presence watching from inside the dream—a shadow figure. My dog again started barking, on the bed this time, and woke me. He was staring out toward the living room and raising hell. My heart was beating fast and I was truly afraid that someone was in the living room. I saw a blue flashing light from my computer monitor that only happens when the computer shuts off. I'd not turned it off, but it was indeed off. My husband woke too and said he had been having a bad dream again. I did go out to the living room to check it out, but other than my computer monitor being off, I could not find anything.

During these two days, while I was at work, my husband was startled twice by our house alarm going off. Nothing was there.

Never has anything like this happened—where I woke frightened and had feelings of someone being in my home who should not be... I'd not called aliens to me, though I had been practicing that process.

What I found out after the fact was that negative entities, aware of their part in Debra's book, were investigating me....in what way, I don't know. Why is this important?

Without realizing it, my nightly ritual of placing protection around my circumstances (my home, my family) had become lax.

I was saying the protection prayer, but it had become routine and was uttered without thinking, without the feeling of connection, just said to get it out of the way so I could get to sleep. Very bad. I was not practicing what I was preaching. Things could have gone very wrong there.

A partner author and psychic medium/artist who was working on a project with me, Salerie, advised me:

> usually, if they want to abduct you, your husband is knocked out and they abduct you; but in your case, they alarmed your husband with a dream so that he could come out and check on you...and also, while you were feeling the out-of-body experience, your dog woke you and you were already saying your protection prayer—which means they didn't get you. It seems there are other entities there that are alerting your dog and your husband whenever they try to mess with you. This sounds to me as if you have major protection...

The take-away here is that when you put up your protection, don't get lazy. Mean it. Your life could depend upon it. It also means that as you move forward with this interior research, you may be calling aliens when you don't realize it. Take care.

DREAMS

This then leads into another way in which star beings visit earthlings: dreams. I usually forget my dreams unless I write them down right away. I tired of that—there were only so many references that made sense. But with the alien visitation, I've found that I remembered them perfectly—well, except for the night they were knocking on my walls (and this new incident I just related in the prior section). So, one of the ways that aliens may visit you is through your dreams.

If you have a dream that you feel is related to the topic, it can be explored via this process, just like an actual, physical, with-your-eyes sighting.

CONCLUSION

I hope sincerely that the conclusion of this book is your beginning down a pathway to understanding the things that may have happened to you, or will in the future occur when it comes to UFO sightings, alien abduction scenarios, or invitational contactee experiences.

Now before you are tempted to say: Is that all there is? I implore you to give this a try. A real try. Once you do, you will find that this method opened up a part of your life that you did not know existed. It's time to do it. Something is coming down the road with our world and this will give you a head's up. This method truly has value.

Remember that if any of the processes I've mentioned feel wrong or you feel that the situation might escalate to something that you are not comfortable with, you have the absolute power to stop. This process is merely a tool. It does take practice to get it right, as with the usage of any tool. Keep detailed records. Do tell someone not involved that your are experimenting in this field...just in case. Be safe in all endeavors.

Manage your experiences always remembering that you are the most important part of the equation.

Happy hunting!

DINAH ROSEBERRY

APPENDIX

PROTECTION PRAYER

May the love of God be with me and in me
And fill me with the white love of love and protection
I come to you in Christ Consciousness,
Come to me in Christ Consciousness.

I ask for the full protection of Lord Michael, the
Archangel of protection.
Lord Michael in front,
Lord Michael behind,
Lord Michael to the right,
Lord Michael to the left,
Lord Michael above,
Lord Michael below,
Lord Michael, Lord Michael wherever I go.

I am His love protecting here.
I am His love protecting here.
I am His love protecting here.

QUESTIONS FOR THOSE WHO BELIEVE THEY HAVE HAD AN EXPERIENCE

1. What are the particulars of the experience: date, time, place?
2. What feelings do I remember having before the experience?
3. What happened during the experience? (Other questions may arise as this description moves forward.)
4. Do I remember the craft and descriptions of the beings present? (Note details.)
5. Do I remember how the incident ended?
6. How did I feel after the event? The next day?
7. Are there ongoing dreams or new encounters related to this one?
8. Have I discussed the situation with someone who understands?
9. Did I learn anything from this encounter? (About myself, about the beings, about the Earth or Universe?)
10. Should I report the incident?

QUESTIONS FOR THOSE WHO DO NOT BELIEVE THEY HAVE HAD AN EXPERIENCE

1. Have I ever had an experience involving a UFO or alien?
2. Have I ever had another reincarnated life when I've had a UFO or alien experience?
3. Am I blocking alien experiences? If so, how? If so, why?
4. If I've had an experience, when did the first one occur?
5. Where did it occur?
6. What were the specifics?
7. Are there gaps or screens of memory that I'm not aware of? What do they entail?
8. Did I learn something from the experience?
9. Was I harmed during the experience?
10. Why was I chosen for the experience?
11. Was the UFO/alien satisfied with the results of the experience?
12. Were/are there others within my family who have also had this experience, specifically related to my personal experience? What are the particulars?

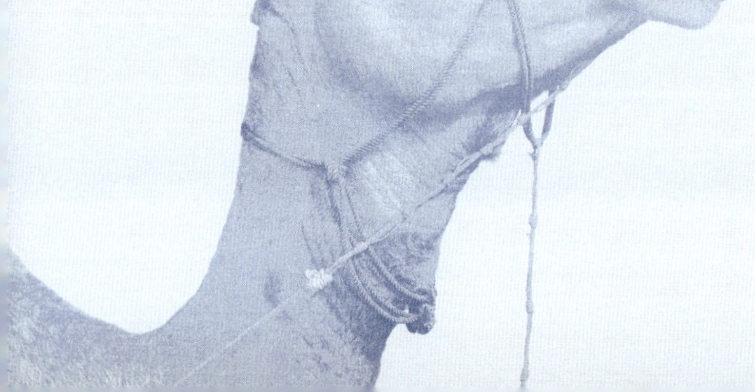

QUESTIONS FOR SOMEONE WHO REMEMBERS AN EXPERIENCE(S), BUT FINDS GAPS IN THEIR MEMORIES

1. When did the first experience occur?

2. Where did it occur?

3. What were the specifics?

4. What are the gaps or screens of memory that I'm not aware of? What do they entail?

5. Did I learn something from the experience?

6. Was I harmed during the experience?

7. Why was I chosen for the experience?

8. Was the UFO/alien satisfied with the results of the experience?

9. Were/are there others within my family who have also had this experience, specifically related to my personal experience? What are the specifics?

QUESTIONS FOR THOSE WISHING TO CONFIRM THE DETAILS OF AN EXPERIENCE

(Similar to the questions for those who believe they've had an experience, but more detailed and usually used at a later time.)

1. When did the first experience occur?
2. Where did it occur?
3. What were the specifics?
4. Are there gaps or screens of memory that I'm not aware of? What do they entail?
5. What did I learn from the experience?
6. Was I harmed during the experience?
7. Why was I chosen for the experience?
8. Was the UFO/alien satisfied with the results of the experience? What did they learn?
9. Were/are there others within my family who have also had this experience, specifically related to my personal experience? What are the specifics?

THE RELAXATION SCRIPT

I will start with my breathing, because my breathing will keep me calm and relaxed throughout my session. To begin, I will take a deep breath in and hold it for three counts—one, two, three—and release it slowly. Now I will tighten all the muscles in my body, then release and relax my muscles. Again, I will tighten all the muscles in my body, then release and relax my muscles. I will take another breath in—one, two, three—and release it. One more time, a breath in—one, two, three—and release.

I will now imagine a bright white light. I see it in the distance moving toward me and I know that this is a healing light, a relaxing light, a protecting light. I see it moving closer to me… and still closer. It is now right in front of me and I notice that there is not only white light, but there are green and yellow swirls of energy going through it. This light will keep me safe as I move into my mind and my experience. It will keep me safe, comfortable, and relaxed. It will never leave me. I will be able to observe everything I intend to look at without fear or worry, because this light will soothe me and keep me safe, and comfortable, and relaxed. This light now moves to me and surrounds me in its pure warm safety. It engulfs me and I soak it in because I know that it will keep me safe, comfortable, and protected, no matter what. It fills my whole body and I can see a glow as I look down at my arms and legs. I see it and feel it.

The only entities that will be able to enter my field of light are those for my highest good. I may interact with my higher self, the masters and guides, and highly evolved loving entities. Any star being that I encounter must respect this white light and come no closer unless allowed by my higher self, my guides, or God. In this way, only those with my highest good can actually touch me. Others may speak to me, but no one can harm me, nothing can upset me because I am only observing at this time. I am totally protected by this pure light.

Now that I have my protective light within me, I notice 10 steps going down to a green and flower-covered valley. I will go down these steps very slowly. Every step downward, I will become ten times more relaxed than I am right now.

One:	*I am so relaxed.*
Two:	*I breathe in and out slowly.*
Three:	*I look down as I move down the steps and see all the beautiful flowers at the bottom of the stairs.*
Four:	*The flowers are all the colors of the rainbow and more.*
Five:	*I see green, and blue, and purple, and pink, and yellow.*
Six:	*The flowers bloom from a vast green meadow.*
Seven:	*I breathe in and out slowly.*
Eight:	*I am more relaxed than I've ever been.*
Nine:	*Relaxed, comfortable, protected.*
Ten:	*I am standing on a path with beautiful flowers all around me.*

THE CLIMB TO MANAGEMENT

(There should be some time given so that the flowers and scenery are enjoyed—about two minutes of quiet should suffice.)

I am standing on the beautiful pathway in the valley and notice that a camel stands to one side. He welcomes me and makes me feel relaxed and safe. He is there to accompany me on my journey. He speaks with me…

(Leave about one minute for the camel to talk. He may speak his name and tell you how he will help you, he may tell you about things he is carrying, he may invite you to ride him, or he may just encourage you in some way.)

The two of us begin our journey by following the flowered pathway. We look at all the colorful flora and we can smell their sweet fragrances. I put my hand on the camel's neck and feel his soft fur. I feel so safe and comfortable and protected with him near. Soon, we see that the pathway is moving upward, climbing the side of the mountain toward the blue sky. The climb is not steep, but goes steadily up. My camel and I are totally relaxed and move up the pathway easily. We notice the trees and shrubbery to the sides of the path—so lush and green. I reach out and touch the rounded leaves of a bush and listen to the buzzing of the insects that comes from within the forest landscape. The sounds are relaxing and I walk forward and upward, enjoying the company of my camel.

(Leave about one minute for the camel to interact.)

We are getting closer to the top of the path that will put us on top the mountain. I can see the puffy clouds in the blue sky and feel the warm sunshine on my face as I climb the path.

I am only a few steps away from reaching the top of the path and will be able to stand on the mountain top, with the clouds and the beautiful sky. I feel my heartbeat speed up just a bit, because I know that there will be someone on top the mountain who will guide me through my first journey. Who will it be? Where will I go?

The camel is moving ahead of me and I'm following him closer and closer to the top. The camel is now disappearing over the top edge of the path onto the mountain top. I am following close behind.

I now see who will be there helping me.

(Leave time for identification of the entity there to help you and a description.)

THE WAY BACK

This part of the visualization process will advise your guide and anyone involved with your experience that you wish to leave and return to full consciousness and into your current life.

I will now be returning to my life, leaving behind any individuals and experiences. However, I will remember each part of my story or experience with perfect clarity.

I am beginning to come back to myself. I tighten and then loosen my muscles. I open my eyes and take in a deep breath. I'm back.

TROUBLESHOOTING

There may be varied circumstances that can cause problems with this process or will require you to do extra added "homework." In some cases, this can't be helped. Do not look at this as a detriment to your success, but as just another rung on the ladder to your management process. Some of these issues could involve the following:

- People who have controlling personalities may have difficulties with visualization and therefore be unable to move through the exercises.

If this is your problem, you will recognize yourself by hearing some of the following statements come out of your mouth: *I can't be hypnotized. I can't visualize anything. I can't relax. This won't work for me.*

You will need to rid yourself of these sentiments first by recognizing that you are trying to control your experiences, rather than understand them, much the way you may control other events in your life. To be successful here, you will need to step away from this program and focus on learning a meditation method (one of your choice). This could take anywhere from two weeks to two years, depending on your intention. It is best to have a mentor or teacher if you intend to move quickly into this program. Having someone work with you will greatly advance your abilities to *let go and let happen*. Once you realize that *allowing* is not a negative thing and that you are not giving up control of anything, you will be able to go back into this program and have successful results. The only holdup to your success is your disallowing it.

- Terror.

If you become terrified at what you uncover, you should seek help from a person who has experience hypnotising those with alien abduction, UFO, and contactee experiences. Do not seek a person who has worked only with hypnotherapy of the normal (clinical) variety. Though they may be qualified, they may not be ready (or knowledgeable) to assist with the kind of help you will need. Author and UFO researcher Debra Marshall advises that though visualization may help you to recall, there needs to be a plan for those who need help afterwards. She has worked with people who were under a type of mind control in the abduction phase and the memory plant was that if the person were to get too close to the truth, they were to hurt themselves (even to the point of suicide as the extreme) to forget the incident again, or to dismiss it as foolishness. This would support Hofer's research that there is something to worry about when working with aliens.

- Blocked.

If you become blocked and can not break through no matter what you do, seek a partner's assistance first; and then, if that does not work, seek (as mentioned prior) a person who has worked with hypnosis dealing with UFOs, etc. That person will know how to go beyond the visualization steps to a deeper hypnotic state. But be advised that even then there are some events that are so heavily screened that it may take years to uncover the reality of your experiences. The question then might be: Do I really want to know?

- You've uncovered other strange phenomena not specifically related to Ufology.

If other types of experiences develop (i.e., paranormal phenomena), feel free to contact investigators in those fields to discuss what you are learning. It will help your management. Be advised that many are finding that there are links between paranormal topics and UFO experiences.

- You are mocked for your beliefs and your efforts.

Ignore anyone who does not take you seriously.

- You are chided for not having the ability to manage your own experiences.

Be cognizant that you are not practicing hypnotism, but are only using visualization as a tool to enter into your own consciousness. Hypnotists you encounter may tell you that you are acting in an irrational or dangerous manner in trying to manage your own mind, but once you explain what you are doing, they will see that this is a visualization experience and that it is a fine prerequisite for hypnosis should you decide to go forward in that direction. Most of you will not need or want to take further steps. Some will. If someone responds negatively to you, understand this—nod politely, and disregard their "well-meaning" advice. I am a hypnotist and I understand these things as well. But I think that in this time of our world, it is more important to be aware of things happening within your own sphere of mind and body than worrying about being able to afford hypnotherapy. Should you have it done professionally? If you can, absolutely. But can you manage some of it yourself? Yes. It's important.

DON'T FORGET!

If at any time you feel uncomfortable, stop.

You should remember that you hold all the power during these experiences. *You* decide what you will remember, recover, catalog, think about, share, believe, etc. If you feel threatened, fearful, uncomfortable, or have any negative feeling as you move through the process, it would be best to take a step back and rethink the steps. Decide what you want to know and what you don't want to know. Discuss your situation with like-minded individuals. You don't have to go it alone.

CASE STUDY 1

The following case studies involve incidents in which I was personally involved. This format for recording your experiences works especially well. A form to work with is available at the back of this book, but making your own is agreeable as long as you capture the information.

For these studies, I did not record via an electronic device and I felt myself several times say: *I'm not going to remember this!* It interrupted my concentration. I do feel that I lost some of the conversation, and again the value of having a recording is emphasized.

Original Date of Experience: 2010?
Session Number: 1
Working Title: Mantis Dream

Special Circumstances: This was a dream that I know was a visitation.

Memories of Incident: There was a knock at the front door. I went to open it and there stood two figures wearing robes and cowls that hid their faces. One was taller than the doorway and the other was about a foot shorter than I (I am 5'5"). They asked if they could come in to talk with me and I agreed. They both sat down on the floor in front of my couch and I sat on the couch's edge, looking at them. I was calm.

I had apparently invited them to visit because I'd wondered about the Mantis group and what they really looked like. They pointed to the glass end table to my left. There was a small revolver on the table. They told me that they were going to lower their cowls for ten seconds only and then they would re-cover their heads. They advised that I would not be able to stand the fear I would feel at their difference in appearance for any longer than that. The gun was there for my calmness. If I became too frightened of them, I was told I could pick up the gun and shoot them. (I felt that they were confident that I would not.)

They lowered the cowls and at this current time I do not remember fear or what they looked like, beyond already knowing of their insect appearance. I did not use the gun or even go for it.

I don't remember the ten seconds.

They re-covered their faces and I asked if they could show my husband. They said that this was not a good time, for my husband was not ready to accept an alien presence in his home. It would be contrary to his thinking or desire.

Date of New Process: August 2013

Special Circumstances: I am choosing to use the process without a partner and to go back to the Mantis visit to glean more data.

Results: The camel took me to the top of the mountain and I was greeted by a very small Grey who offered a hand to me. I took it and then was suddenly back in my living room the night I was visited by the Mantis pair. They knocked, entered, and sat on the floor as before. They showed their faces for ten seconds as before. All was the same.

But then I found that there was more conversation than I'd remembered. I was told that I was part of a specific group (like a team) that encompassed many different individuals. That everyone in humanity belonged to such a team. I asked if there were other humans in my group—they said I could call it a soul group for lack of a different word. I and Preston Dennett [an author in California whom I'd worked with for some years and who has written the testimonial for this book] were the only two humans in this group. Others I knew (friends, family, coworkers) were in other groups.

They said that I did not have the confidence in my abilities to interact with the group to have deeper experiences, i.e., having physical contact that would be remembered. But that I was getting closer to it.

There were hours of conversation about all kinds of things, but this was all they wanted to relay to my conscious mind at this time.

One thing that was relayed that was independent of the discussion between the two Mantis figures, had to do with the Light Beings. They remained at my left side throughout the encounter and oversaw the situation. They wanted me to know that they would be there at every meeting and I would never be left to feign for myself in any way. They noted that some of the group in which I belonged were quite alien to anything I would be able to imagine and that they would act as a buffer for as long as I needed such a thing.

I was then back with the small Grey, who took me back to my camel. Down the path I went until suddenly I was conscious again.

The trip felt as though it was about five minutes long. In "real time" it was thirty minutes.

CASE STUDY 2

Original Date of Experience: Summer 2009?
Session Number: 2
Working Title: Past-life Experience. Flood.

Special Circumstances: I asked if there were past lives where I'd had UFO experiences and was advised that yes, this was true.

Memories of Incident: I'd been regressed in approximately 2009 to a time when I was a native woman living in Mexico. I was important in the tribe. (There is a full regression scenario, but it does not need to be discussed here, as the mention of it is only to show that this is the past life that I would be shown in the visualization that follows.)

Date of New Process: August 2013

Special Circumstances: I am choosing to use the process without a partner during a meditative state as research for this book.

Results: I was joined at the top of the mountain by a small Zeta (Grey) again—he was the same one as in my first case study. We discussed the development of a management group that others could take advantage of and I was given ideas.

I was then shown a landscape that reflected my prior past-life regression. There were many tribal members moving around a community setting. There with me was a Zeta-like individual, but not the typical Grey. This one looked more like the "good" alien from the television program *Fallen Skies*. I found that interesting and mentioned it. He told me that the vision he projected was to keep me from being afraid. This was a familiar positive image for me, so he'd chosen it. I just nodded.

I was shown the tribe working in their camp. Then they were all pointing to the sky, seeing a saucer-like UFO. Suddenly, they all gently fell to the ground asleep. The guide told me that there would be a flood in this area and if the camp were not moved, they would all die. They would intervene to see that this did not happen. So the entire camp, down to their homes and every possession, were moved further inland. I was told that the tribe would have no memory of the move. Then the people awoke and went about their business as though nothing were different.

FORMS

UFO and Alien Management Report
Original Date of Experience:
Session Number:
Working Title:
Special Circumstances:
Memories of Incident:

Date of New Process:
Special Circumstances:
Results:

RESOURCES

Arcturi.com: Aliens, UFOs, Arcturians, and More. http://arcturi.com/ArcturianArchives/ArcturianOrigins.html. Accessed 6/29/2013.

Bashar's Lab. www.bashar.com. Accessed 6/29/13.

Discovery Education. http://school.discoveryeducation.com/schooladventures/universe/itsawesome/lightyears. Accessed 6/29/2013.

Hawking, Stephen. "Humans Should Fear Aliens." *Huffington Post*. Accessed 6/27/2013

Ravy,Villard. "It's Fun to Believe in Weird Things." *Discover News*. Accessed 6/27/2013

What is known about certain alien species? http://www.noufors.com/ Accessed 6/29/2013.

www.dictionary.com. Accessed 6/29/13.

Zeta Talk. www.zetatalk.com. Accessed daily.

RECOMMENDED READING

Mid-Atlantic UFOs: High Traffic Area
Gerard Medvec
978-0-7643-4507-4

Evolutionary Ufology
Jordan Hofer
ISBN: 978-0-7643-4505-0

Midwest UFOs and Beyond
Tom Baker
ISBN: 978-0-7643-4390-2

Alien Encounters in the Western United States
Tracie Austin
ISBN: 978-0-7643-4145-8

Supernatural Arkansas: Ghosts, Monsters, and the Unexplained
Alan Lowe and Jason Hall
ISBN: 978-0-7643-4123-6

UFOs Above Pennsylvania
Mark Sarro and Gerard Medvec
ISBN: 978-0-7643-4292-9

UFOs Above the Law: True Encounters with Law Enforcement
Frank Soriano & Jim Bouck
ISBN: 978-0-7643-3920-2

UFOs in Missouri: True Tales of Extraterrestrials and Related Phenomena
Lee Prosser
ISBN: 978-0-7643-3747-5

UFOs Over California: A True History of Extraterrestrial Encounters in the Golden State
Preston Dennett
ISBN: 978-0-7643-2149-8

UFOs Over New Mexico: A True History of Extraterrestrial Encounters in the Land of Enchantment
Preston Dennett
ISBN: 978-0-7643-3906-6

UFOs Over New York: A True History of Extraterrestrial Encounters in the Empire State
Preston Dennett
ISBN: 978-0-7643-2974-6

UFO Conspiracy
Carmen McLaren
ISBN: 978-0-7643-3893-9

New Jersey UFOs
Gerard J. Medvec
ISBN: 978-0-7643-4622-4

UFOs Over Maine
Nomar Slevik
ISBN: 978-0-7643-4623-1

The Ra Material: Law of One
Jim McCarty & Carla L. Rueckert
5 volumes and ISBNs

A Silent Invasion: The Truth About Aliens, Alien Abductions, and UFOs
Rev. Debra Marshall
ISBN: 978-0-7643-4609-5

WEBSITES TO STUDY

www.zetatalk.com
Channeled by Nancy Leider. Touches every area of ufology from the Grey perspective. Planet X news.

http://drboylan.com/
Dr. Richard Boylan's Star Seed program and excellent description of varied alien races.

http://betseylewis.com/Earth_News_1.html
Betsey Lewis, author, radio show host. This is the best newsletter for keeping abreast of anything otherworldly or that affects our planet.